Franz LISZT

PROMETHEUS
Symphonic Poem No. 5
S. 97

Study Score
Partitur

PETRUCCI LIBRARY PRESS

INTRODUCTION

The present score is a reissue of one from the Franz Liszt-Stiftung edition, originally published by Breitkopf & Härtel from 1907-1936. The edition was prepared in an effort to publish the entire oeuvre of Franz Liszt. Editors included such prominent musicians as Béla Bartok, Ferruccio Busoni, Eugène d'Albert and José Vianna da Motta – some of whom studied with Liszt – as well as scholars like Peter Raabe, who would later compile the first catalog of the composer's works. The need for a complete edition was already apparent by the time of Liszt's death. Although some of his piano music had regularly appeared in new editions throughout his life, these works were by no means representative of even his pianistic output. A far more unfortunate fate was left for his orchestral music - which would usually be issued only once, soon to go out of print and later scarcely available. The Liszt-Stiftung edition revived many works that had fallen into relative obscurity and was therefore handsomely welcomed.

The edition was sadly never completed. The publication activity was brought to a premature end by the time of the Second World War. All in all the incomplete edition encompassed 34 volumes, among others two symphonies, the symphonic poems, some concert works, a couple of piano arrangements and 11 volumes of original works for piano – a mere fraction of the composer's output – but the edition would nonetheless break the ground for Liszt research during the 20th century for a number of reasons. First, it brought to light a number of late pieces that would put Liszt as a forerunner of experimental music and firmly establish his position as such. Second, it revealed the diversity of Liszt's output, which up until that time had been best known as an important addition to the piano repertoire. Third, it displayed the complex and characteristic nature of many of his works by being the first edition to show and make use of several alternative (sometimes vastly different) versions and sources. Last but not least, it would provide the world with a generally reliable edition of easy availability and very high standard for its day.

The Bavarian State Library acquired a complete copy of said edition and decided to digitize it in 2008. By that time more than 70 years had passed since its publication, effectively rendering the edition out of copyright and free for any use. Each and every page was scanned and uploaded to their online digital collection. While this was a great effort in itself, the site has a rudimentary interface, is difficult to navigate and the scores are not in the context of relevant information. One of our users decided to also upload it to our site, the International Music Score Library Project (IMSLP) / Petrucci Music Library, the unique wiki-based repository of musical scores, composers and indexes that anyone can edit and amend. Through the effort of a single user, Mattias K. (piupianissimo), the entire edition is now easily

available worldwide to those who wish to perform and study the composer's music in a historical context, since as the case is with Liszt's music, many early editions exist and many are readily available on the site and many more will be available in the future. IMSLP is as such a valuable resource available to the scholar but even more to the performer who is always a mere mouse click away from scores that have not been in print since the turn of the past century, or that are otherwise hard to come by. The availability, quantity of ease of access for online scores will soon exceed those of the traditional medium of print. Nevertheless new works have always been published through the printed medium and this tradition is going to persist for many years to come even if complemented by the digital medium. Of course an important fact to stress is that the availability of digital scores online does not exclude the need of printed score since neither one can replace the comfort and neatness of one another. The quality of a bound reprint or new engraving exceeds that of a score printed at home.

I discovered IMSLP back in early 2006 when it first began. At that time many scores were scattered on the net either privately or on commercial collection sites. Many of these sites had a considerably large collection but sadly many had restrictions on number of downloads per day and the process of contributing to them was riddled with bureaucracy. IMSLP was the first free site where anyone could contribute and upload any kind of musical scores. I have personally searched and uploaded many works – particularly those of Liszt – and the future of the site is nothing but bright. At the time of its start only a handful of scores were available on the site but through the effort of its users IMSLP has grown to be the largest collection of scores available on the Internet.

Prometheus is the fifth work in a series of thirteen symphonic poems composed by Franz Liszt. It was composed from 1855 and first published in 1856 by Breitkopf und Härtel of Leipzig. The dedicatee is Princess Carolyne zu Sayn-Wittgenstein. This score is from the second volume of the Franz Liszt-Stiftung edition, edited by Otto Taubmann and published in 1909. The score, along with a number or arrangements, is also available directly at the following URL:

http:// imslp.org/wiki/Prometheus,_S.99_(Liszt,_Franz)

Soren Afshar (Funper)

Summer, 2011

COMPOSER'S PREFACE

Eine Aufführung, welche den Intentionen des Komponisten entsprechen und ihnen Klang, Farbe, Rhythmus und Leben verleihen soll, wird bei meinen Orchester-Werken am zweckmässigsten und mit dem geringsten Zeitverlust durch geteilte Vor-Proben gefördert werden. Demzufolge erlaube ich mir, die HH. Dirigenten, welche meine symphonischen Dichtungen aufzuführen beabsichtigen, zu ersuchen, der General-Probe Separat-Proben mit dem Streich-Quartett, andere mit Blas- und Schlag-Instrumenten vorangehen zu lassen.

Gleichzeitig sei mir gestattet zu bemerken, dass ich das mechanische, taktmässige, zerschnittene Auf- und Abspielen, wie es an manchen Orten noch üblich ist, möglichst beseitigt wünsche, und nur den periodischen Vortrag, mit dem Hervortreten der besonderen Accente und der Abrundung der melodischen und rhythmischen Nuanzierung, als sachgemäss anerkennen kann. In der geistigen Auffassung des Dirigenten liegt der Lebensnerv einer symphonischen Produktion, vorausgesetzt, dass im Orchester die geziemenden Mittel zu deren Verwirklichung sich vorfinden; andernfalls möchte es ratsamer erscheinen, sich nicht mit Werken zu befassen, welche keineswegs eine Alltags-Popularität beanspruchen.

Obschon ich bemüht war, durch genaue Anzeichnungen meine Intentionen zu verdeutlichen, so verhehle ich doch nicht, dass Manches, ja sogar das Wesentlichste, sich nicht zu Papier bringen lässt, und nur durch das künstlerische Vermögen, durch sympathisch schwungvolles Reproduzieren, sowohl des Dirigenten als der Aufführenden, zur durchgreifenden Wirkung gelangen kann. Dem Wohlwollen meiner Kunstgenossen sei es daher überlassen, das Meiste und Vorzüglichste an meinen Werken zu vollbringen.

Weimar, März 1856.

Pour obtenir un résultat d'exécution correspondant aux intentions de mes œuvres orchestrales, et leur donner le coloris, le rhythme, l'accent et la vie qu'elles réclament, il sera utile d'en préparer la répétition générale par des répétitions partielles des instruments à cordes, à vent, en cuivre, et à percussion. Par cette méthode de la division du travail on épargnera du temps en facilitant aux exécutants l'intelligence de l'ouvrage. Je me permets en conséquence de prier MM. les chefs d'orchestre qui seraient disposés à faire exécuter l'un de ces Poèmes symphoniques, de vouloir bien prendre le soin de faire précéder les répétitions générales, des répétitions préalables indiquées ci-dessus.

En même temps j'observerai que la mesure dans les œuvres de ce genre demande à être maniée avec plus de mesure, de souplesse, et d'intelligence des effets de coloris, de rhythme, et d'expression qu'il n'est encore d'usage dans beaucoup d'orchestres. Il ne suffit pas qu'une composition soit régulièrement bâtonnée et machinalement exécutée avec plus ou moins de correction pour que l'auteur ait à se louer de cette façon de propagation de son œuvre, et puisse y reconnaître une fidèle interprétation de sa pensée. Le nerf vital d'une belle exécution symphonique gît principalement dans la compréhension de l'œuvre reproduite, que le chef d'orchestre doit surtout posséder et communiquer, dans la manière de partager et d'accentuer les périodes, d'accuser les contrastes tout en ménageant les transitions de veiller tantôt à établir l'équilibre entre les divers instruments, tantôt à les faire ressortir soit isolément soit par groupes, car à tel moment il convient d'entonner ou de marquer simplement les notes, mais à d'autres il s'agit de phraser, de chanter, et même de déclamer. C'est au chef qu'il appartient d'indiquer à chacun des membres de l'orchestre la signification du rôle qu'il a à remplir.

Je me suis attaché à rendre mes intentions par rapport aux nuances, à l'accélération et au retard des mouvements, etc. aussi sensibles que possible par un emploi détaillé des signes et des expressions usitées; néanmoins ce serait une illusion de croire qu'on puisse fixer sur le papier ce qui fait la beauté et le caractère de l'exécution. Le talent et l'inspiration des artistes dirigeants et exécutants en ont seuls le secret, et la part de sympathie que ceux-ci voudront bien accorder à mes œuvres, seront pour elles le meilleur gage de succès.

Weimar, Mars 1856.

In order to secure a performance of my orchestral works which accords with their intentions, and which imparts to them the colour, rhythm, accent and life that they require, it is recommended that the general rehearsal should be preceded by separate rehearsals of the Strings, Wind, Brass, and instruments of percussion. By this division of labour time will be saved, and the executants will more rapidly be made familiar with what is required of them. I therefore venture to request that conductors, who are pleased to bring one or the other of my symphonic poems to a hearing will adopt the plan formulated above.

At the same time I may be allowed to remark that it is my wish that the mechanical, bar by bar, up and down beating of time, which obtains in so many places, should as far as possible be discarded, and that only the periodic divisions, with the prominence of certain accentuation and the rounding off of melodic and rhythmical nuances should alone be regarded as indispensable. The vitality of a symphonic performance depends upon the intellectual perception of the conductor, presuming that suitable material for its realisation is to be found in the orchestra; failing this it would seem to be advisable to hold aloof from works which do not claim a promise of every-day popularity.

Although I have endeavoured to make my intentions clear by providing exact marks of expression, I cannot conceal from myself that much, and that perhaps the most important, cannot be set forth on paper, but can only be successfully brought to light by the artistic capability and the sympathetic and enthusiastic reproduction by both conductor and executants. It may therefore be left to my colleagues in art to do the most and best that they can for my works.

Weimar, March 1856.

F. Liszt.

PROMETHEUS
SYMPHONISCHE DICHTUNG Nr. 5 VON F. LISZT.

Die Enthüllung der Statue Herders fand im Jahre 1850 in Weimar statt und der betreffende Tag sollte durch eine Theatervorstellung gefeiert werden, welche speziell der Verehrung dieses poetischen Denkers gewidmet war. Unter seinen Kantaten und Gedichten in dramatischer Form wählten wir den entfesselten Prometheus, — eines seiner Werke dieser Gattung, aus welchem am reinsten die Lauterkeit und der Seelenadel dieses Mannes hervorleuchtet, welchen man den Apostel der Humanität nannte — um die lyrischen Partien daraus in Musik zu setzen, zu welchem Zweck sie ursprünglich gedichtet waren. Der vorliegenden Komposition, welche als Ouvertüre diente, fügten wir Chöre zu, die wir uns vorbehalten, später zu einem bühnen- oder konzertmässigen Ensemble zu vereinigen, da die damalige Vorstellung eine ausnahmsweise war, indem man, um die Gedanken und das Werk des grossen Philosophen unangetastet zu lassen, seinen Text im Ganzen wiedergab, so wenig er unsren bestehenden dramatischen Anforderungen entspricht.

Der Prometheus-Mythus ist voll mysteriöser Ideen, dunkler Traditionen, voll Hoffnungen, deren Berechtigung immer bezweifelt wird, so lebendig sie im Gefühl leben. In mehrfacher Weise gedeutet von den gelehrten und poetischen Exegesen der verschiedensten Überzeugungen und Negationen, spricht dieser Mythus immer lebhaft zur bewegten Einbildungskraft durch geheime Übereinstimmungen seiner Symbolik mit unsren beharrlichsten Instinkten, unsren herbsten Schmerzen und beseligendsten Ahnungen. Die antiken Bildwerke tun uns kund, wie sehr die erregte Fantasie der griechischen Kunst sich mit ihm beschäftigte. Wie die Poesie sich in diesen Gegenstand vertiefte, zeigt uns das Fragment des Aeschylus. Wir brauchten nicht unter den verschiedenen Auslegungen zu wählen, welche sich reichlich um diese erhabenen Monumente angesammelt haben, noch auch die antike Legende mit ihren reichen Anklängen an alte, dunkle Erinnerungen, unvergängliche, ewige Hoffnungen in

PROMÉTHÉE
POÈME SYMPHONIQUE No. 5 DE F. LISZT.

L'inauguration de la statue de Herder eut lieu à Weimar en 1850, et à ce jour la représentation théâtrale fut spécialement consacrée au souvenir de ce poète-penseur. D'entre toutes ses cantates et poésies quasi dramatiques, nous avions choisi le Prométhée délivré, une des œuvres de ce genre où se traduit le mieux ce qu'il y avait de plus pur et de plus généreux dans les sentiments de celui qui fut appelé l'apôtre de l'Humanité, — pour y adapter quelques morceaux de chant, cet ouvrage ayant été originairement destiné à être mis en musique. Outre la partition présente qui servit d'ouverture, nous en avons composé les chœurs, que nous nous réservons de relier plus tard en un ensemble, d'exécution plus usuelle sur les théâtres ou dans les concerts que celle qui eut lieu alors, où, pour ne rien toucher à la pensée et à l'œuvre de l'illustre philosophe, son texte fut déclamé dans son entier, quelque peu approprié qu'il fût à nos habitudes dramatiques actuelles.

Le mythe de Prométhée est plein de mystérieuses idées, de vagues traditions, d'espoirs aussi dénués de corps que vivaces de sentiment. Interprété de plus d'une façon par les savantes et poétiques exégèses de croyances et de négations aussi convaincues qu'opposées entre elles, il a toujours parlé à l'imagination émue par les secrètes concordances de ce symbolique récit avec nos instincts les plus opiniâtres, avec nos douleurs les plus âcres, avec nos pressentiments les plus doux. Les marbres antiques nous montrent combien il préoccupait la rêverie inquiète de l'art grec; le fragment d'Eschyle nous prouve que la poésie y trouvait un profond sujet de méditation. Nous n'avons pas eu à choisir entre tant de gloses accumulées autour de ses sublimes monuments, ni à gréer une variante nouvelle à cette antique légende, si apparentée à d'antiques et confus souvenirs, à d'éternelles et toujours jeunes espérances. Il suffit à la musique de s'assimiler les sentiments qui, sous toutes

PROMETHEUS
SYMPHONIC POEM No. 5 by F. LISZT.

It seemed well that the unveiling of a statue to the memory of Herder, which took place at Weimar in 1850, should be followed on the same day by a theatrical representation especially designed in honour of this poetical thinker. From amongst his cantatas and dramatic poems I therefore made choice of the "Prometheus Unbound", as being one of those of his works which best represents the pure and generous in the character of him, who has been called "the Apostle of humanity", with the view of setting its lyrical portions to music, as he originally intended should be done. I supplemented the present work, which served as overture, with choruses, but reserved them for some future stage or concert performance, the occasion alluded to being quite an exceptional one, at which, in order to leave the thought and work of this great philosopher intact, the text, little as it accords with our dramatic requirements, was declaimed in its integrity.

The Prometheus myth is full of mystic ideas, vague traditions, and hopes as unlikely to be realised, as they are lively in sentiment. Interpreted in several ways by the learned and poetical commentators on the most opposite convictions and negations, this myth has always in the liveliest manner appealed to the imagination by its hidden symbolical accordance with our strongest instincts, our bitterest sorrows, and our happiest forebodings. The statues of antiquity show us how deeply it excited and engaged the fancy of Greek art; the fragment of Aeschylus proves that Poetry regarded it as a profound subject for meditation. There was no need to choose between the many interpretations which these sublime monuments had provoked, nor to mould afresh this antique legend, which so strongly re-echoes dim reminiscences, imperishable and eternal hopes. It was sufficient to translate into music those phases of feeling, which, under the repeatedly varied forms of the myth,

neuer Weise zu gestalten. Es genügte, in der Musik die Stimmungen aufgehen zu lassen, welche unter den verschiedenen wechselnden Formen des Mythus seine Wesenheit, gleichsam seine Seele, bilden: Kühnheit, Leiden, Ausharren, Erlösung. Kühnes Hinanstreben nach den höchsten Zielen, welche dem menschlichen Geiste erreichbar scheinen, Schaffensdrang, Tätigkeitstrieb... Sündentilgende Schmerzen, welche unablässig an dem Lebensnerv unsres Daseins nagen, ohne es zu zerstören; Verurteilung, angeschmiedet zu sein an den öden Uferfelsen unsrer irdischen Natur; Angstrufe und blutige Tränen.... Aber ein unentreissbares Bewusstsein angeborner Grösse und künftiger Erlösung; untilgbarer Glaube an einen Befreier, welcher den langgequälten Gefangenen emporheben wird zu den überirdischen Regionen, denen er den lichten Funken entwandte, und endlich... Vollendung des Werkes der Gnade, wenn der ersehnte Tag gekommen.

Leid und Verklärung! So zusammengedrängt erheischte die Grundidee dieser nur zu wahren Fabel einen gewitterschwülen, sturmgrollenden Ausdruck. Ein tiefer Schmerz, der durch trotzbietendes Ausharren triumphiert, bildet den musikalischen Charakter dieser Vorlage. (Übers. v. P. Cornelius.)

les formes successivement imposées à ce mythe, en ont fait le fond et comme l'âme: Audace, Souffrance, Endurance, et Salvation: aspiration hardie vers les plus hautes destinées que l'esprit humain puisse aborder; activité créatrice, besoin d'expansion .... douleurs expiatoires livrant à un rongement incessant nos organes vitaux, sans nous anéantir; condamnation à un dur enchaînement sur les plus arides plages de notre nature: cris d'angoisse et larmes de sang ... mais inamissible conscience d'une grandeur native, d'une future délivrance; foi tacite en un libérateur qui fera monter le captif longtemps torturé aux régions transmondaines dont il dérobait la lumineuse étincelle ... et enfin, l'accomplissement de l'œuvre de miséricorde, le grand jour venu!

Malheur et Gloire! ainsi resserrée, la pensée fondamentale de cette trop véridique fable, ne se prêtait qu'à une expression orageuse, fulgurante dirions-nous. Une désolation triomphante par la persévérance de la hautaine énergie forme le caractère musical de cette donnée. F. Liszt.

together constitute its entirety, its soul: viz; Boldness, Suffering, Endurance, and Redemption. Bold striving after the highest destiny, to which the human spirit can aspire, creative activity, the necessity for action ... expiating pains, which unceasingly gnaw at the fundamental source of our being, without destroying it; condemnation to be fettered on the barren cliffs of our earthly nature; cries of anguish and tears of blood... on the other hand, an inalienable Consciousness of inborn greatness and future redemption; inextinguishable faith in a deliverer, who shall raise the long-tortured prisoner to the supermundane regions, which he robbed of the luminous spark, and finally... the accomplishment of a work of grace, when the longed for day has come.

Suffering and Apotheosis! Thus compressed, the fundamental idea of this too truthful fable demanded a sultry, stormy and tempestuous mode of expression. A desolating grief, triumphing at last by energy and preseverance, constitutes the musical character of the piece now offered to notice.

After the 1854 relief by Ernst Rietschel

INSTRUMENTATION

2 Flutes
Piccolo
2 Oboes
English Horn
2 Clarinets (C)
2 Bassoons

4 Horns (E)
2 Trumpets (C)
3 Trombones
Tuba

Timpani

Violins I
Violins II
Violas
Violoncellos
Basses

Duration: ca. 12 minutes

First Performance: October 18, 1855
Braunschweig: Orchestra
Franz Liszt, conductor

ISBN: 978-1-60874-025-3

This score is an unabridged reprint of the score
first issued in Leipzig by Breitkopf & Härtel, 1908. Plate F.L. 5

Printed in the USA
First Printing: November, 2011

PROMETHEUS

Symphonic Poem No. 5

S. 99

Franz Liszt (1811–1886)

PETRUCCI LIBRARY PRESS

Andante. (Recitativo.)

8

10

16

18

21

22

28

H poco a poco accelerando il tempo (sin' al Allegro agitato assai).

30

32

34

38

Tempo primo (Allegro energico ed agitato assai).

40

Andante (Recitativo).

Andante (Recitativo).

Zur Kürzung des Stückes.
To shorten the piece.
Pour abréger le morceau.

43

44

46

48

54

55

58

66

FRANZ LISZTS SYMPHONISCHE DICHTUNGEN 5 u. 6

REVISIONSBERICHT

Im Jahre 1908 wurden in einer gemeinschaftlichen Sitzung der Revisoren, der Herausgeber und der Verleger die Leitgedanken und Grundsätze für eine vollständige, einheitliche und korrekte Gesamtausgabe der Werke Franz Liszts beraten und endgültig festgesetzt.

Aus praktischen Gründen der modernen Musikpflege mußten die vielfachen Unterschiede in der Benennung und Anordnung der Instrumente, in den Schlüsseln usw., vor allem aber sehr viele, für heutige Begriffe überflüssige oder selbst störende Versetzungszeichen beseitigt werden. Die auf letztere bezügliche Bestimmung lautet in endgültiger Fassung:

»Die von Liszt sehr reichlich angewendeten zufälligen Versetzungszeichen (namentlich Auflösungszeichen) sind für die heutige Praxis zum Teil entbehrlich geworden. Die nicht unbedingt notwendigen sind nur da beizubehalten, wo sie das Lesen tatsächlich noch erleichtern, Mißverständnisse verhüten oder für das harmonische Bild Lisztscher Schreibweise besonders charakteristisch erscheinen.«

Um jede Willkür auszuschliessen, sind alle irgendwie nennenswerten Änderungen, Weglassungen, Zusätze im Wortlaut der Lisztschen Partitur im Revisionsbericht je bei der betreffenden Komposition besonders aufgeführt und begründet worden, sodaß jeder mit der alten und der neuen Ausgabe in der Hand sich sein Urteil selbst bilden kann. Alle Zutaten, insbesondere Vortragsbezeichnungen, wurden in Klammern ( ) oder [ ] gesetzt; in einzelnen Fällen kann und soll dies nachträglich noch geschehen.

Die Herausgabe der Symphonischen Dichtungen war ursprünglich von Herrn Eugen d'Albert übernommen worden, der jedoch wegen anderweitiger großer Inanspruchnahme zurücktrat, nachdem er den Stich aller 12 Werke nur in erster Lesung hatte beaufsichtigen können. Die genaue Nachprüfung übernahm in dankenswerter Weise Herr Otto Taubmann in Berlin, in stetem Einvernehmen mit dem Kustos des Liszt-Museums, Herrn Hofrat Dr. Obrist, als dem Obmann der Revisionskommission.

BAND 3

PROMETHEUS.
Symphonische Dichtung Nr. 5.

Vorlage: Die erste Partiturausgabe, erschienen 1856 bei Breitkopf & Härtel in Leipzig. Verlagsnummer 9191.

Bemerkungen:

S. 9. Die gedruckte Vorlage hat im ersten Takt auf dem dritten Taktviertel in der zweiten Hälfte der II. Violinen die Note *d*, die als Fehler zu erachten ist; die Fortschreitung ergibt falsche Oktaven mit dem Baß. Es dürfte, wie ein Vergleich mit der analogen Stelle auf S. 41, Takt 3 ergibt, ein Stichfehler vorliegen, der durch Änderung des *d* in *h* beseitigt wurde.

S. 44, Takt 4 haben die II. Violinen in der gedruckten Vorlage vom 6. bis zum 8. Achtel ein Diminuendozeichen (>), die rhythmisch mitgehenden Violoncelle und Bässe über der Viertelnote aber nur ein Marcatozeichen (·). Da bei der analogen Stelle auf S. 9, 2. Takt auch in den II. Violinen nur das Marcatozeichen steht, wurde > auf S. 44 als Stichfehler der Vorlage erachtet und in ein Marcatozeichen umgeändert.

S. 51 hat die gedruckte Vorlage im 6. bis 8. Takt für die zusammengehenden Fagotte und 1. Horn verschiedene dynamische Vorschriften, die in Übereinstimmung mit einander gebracht wurden.

* * *

MAZEPPA.
Symphonische Dichtung Nr. 6.

Vorlage: Die erste Partiturausgabe, erschienen 1856 bei Breitkopf & Härtel in Leipzig. Verlagsnummer 9137.

Bemerkungen:

S. 8, 4. Takt
S. 9, 2. u. 4. Takt } wurden die < unter den Bläsern auf gleiche Länge mit denen unter den Streichern gebracht.

S. 9, 2. Takt hat die *D*-Klarinette in der gedruckten Vorlage *ais*, während *b* sowohl der Vorzeichnung wie der Stimmführung (*as-b-c*) nach als viel natürlicher erscheint. Wurde demgemäß geändert.

S. 18, 1. u. 2. Takt wurde das > in Fagotten, Hörnern und Posaunen gemäß der analogen Stelle auf S. 17, 1. und 2. Takt, bis zum angebundenen Achtel verlängert.

S. 34, 1. Takt ff. und S. 43, 1. Takt ff. ist in der gedruckten Vorlage die Bezeichnung der Violoncellstimmen zweifelhaft. Unter den Triolen des 3. Viertels steht (gleichzeitig mit der entsprechenden Bezeichnung in der zweiten Hälfte der II. Violinen und in den Bratschen) »*col legno*«. Da die Bezeichnung nicht wiederholt wird, würde sie bis zur Aufhebung ihrer Bedeutung durch eine andere Vorschrift in Geltung zu bleiben haben. Dem widerspricht aber, daß das erste Viertel im ersten dieser Takte nicht »*col legno*« gespielt werden soll. Da nun die nächsten Takte eine ständige Wiederholung des rhythmischen Motivs

| ♩ 𝄾 ♫♫ 𝄾 | ♫♫ 𝄾 - |

bringen, wurde angenommen, daß es der Absicht des Komponisten entspreche, wenn stets nur die beiden Triolen »*col legno*«, das vorangehende Viertel aber jedesmal mit Bogenstrich gegeben werde.

S. 58, 7. Takt
S. 59, 1., 3., 5., 7. Takt } Die Zeichen × × über den Akkorden in den Streichern bedeuten, laut diesbezüglichen Anmerkungen in den Orchesterstimmen, daß diese Akkorde *pizzicato* gespielt werden sollen.
S. 60, 1., 3. Takt

* * *

www.ingramcontent.com/pod-product-compliance
Lightning Source LLC
Chambersburg PA
CBHW081348040426
42450CB00015B/3354